CLASSIC *f*M

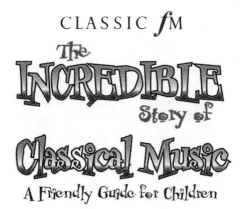

The
INCREDIBLE
Story of
Classical Music
A Friendly Guide for Children

CLASSIC *f*M

The
INCREDIBLE
Story of
Classical Music
A Friendly Guide for Children

DARREN HENLEY

HODDER
EDUCATION
PART OF HACHETTE LIVRE UK

Cover illustration: Oxford Designers and Illustrators

The publisher has used its best endeavours to ensure that the URLs for external websites referred to in this book are correct and active at the time of going to press. However, the publisher has no responsibility for the websites and can give no guarantee that a site will remain live or that the content is or will remain appropriate.

For UK order enquiries: please contact Bookpoint Ltd, 130 Milton Park, Abingdon, Oxon OX14 4SB. Telephone: +44(0) 1235 827720. Fax: +44(0) 1235 400454. Lines are open 09.00–17.00, Monday to Saturday, with a 24-hour message answering service. You can also order through our website www.hoddereducation.com

British Library Cataloguing in Publication Data: a catalogue record for this title is available from the British Library.

First published in UK 2008, by Hodder Education, part of Hachette Livre UK, 338 Euston Road, London NW1 3BH.

Copyright © 2008 Darren Henley

Typeset by Servis Filmsetting Ltd, Stockport, Cheshire
Printed in Great Britain for Hodder Education, a division of Hachette Livre UK, 338 Euston Road, London NW1 3BH, by CPI Cox & Wyman, Reading, Berkshire, RG1 8EX.

Hachette Livre UK's policy is to use papers that are natural, renewable and recyclable products and made from wood grown in sustainable forests. The logging and manufacturing processes are expected to conform to the environmental regulations of the country of origin.

ISBN   978 0 340 98357 7

Impression number   10 9 8 7 6 5 4 3

Year   2011 2010 2009 2008

Contents

CLARENCE HOUSE

There is no reason why classical music shouldn't be part of everyone's life. The tradition, stories and emotional power of classical music are available and accessible to everyone.

The Incredible Story of Classical Music is full of stories about some of the most beautiful music ever written – the people who wrote it; the places where they lived; the things that they did. I hope it will help you find your way around the history of classical music and, more importantly, that it will help you to find pieces of music that you love.

When I was young, I heard Jacqueline du Pré play the 'cello. I can still remember her performance clearly and, indeed, it inspired me to start to learn the 'cello myself. Music has always been important to me – enjoying music, whether as a listener or as a music-maker, seems to me to be as basic a human activity as laughter.

All of the profits from the sale of The Incredible Story of Classical Music are going to support my Foundation for Children & the Arts, which gives thousands of children each year a chance to discover music – and all the arts – for themselves. Thank you for helping us by buying this book.

Welcome to The Incredible Story of Classical Music

Have you ever imagined what the world would be like if we had no music at all? To find out, try holding this book very, very still indeed. Don't say a single word to anyone – not even to yourself.

Instead, just listen.

Can you hear how very quiet it is in here now?

Don't worry, though. This isn't a quiet book at all.

In fact, it's filled with stories about the most beautiful and exciting sounds ever made. As you read it, you'll find out all about the incredible people who made these incredible sounds in the first place. You'll also discover some of the greatest pieces of classical music ever written.

Happy reading! And happy listening too!

It's interesting to read about classical music, but it's far more fun to actually listen to it. We've got together with iTunes to create a special playlist of some of the music included in our **Incredible Story**. You can listen to excerpts of each of these pieces online for free and you can also buy them in full and download them onto your iPod.

 To find out more, go online to www.classicfm.com/incredible and look out for this symbol throughout our **Incredible Story**.

There is a full list of all the music featured in this book on pages 98–103.

The Five Stages of Classical Music

Over the next hundred or so pages, you'll discover that there are five different stages in classical music's history.

The first is called the **Early Music Period** and it includes all of the music written before the year 1600.

The next stage of classical music is called the **Baroque Period** and it includes the music composed between 1600 and 1750.

Confusingly, the third stage of classical music is known as the **Classical Period**. It ran from around 1750 to roughly 1830. Don't panic about getting this muddled up!

The **Romantic Period** followed and it includes the music written from around

1830 through until the start of the 20th century in 1900.

Our final stage includes all of the classical music written in the last hundred or so years, from 1900 onwards. We call this **20th and 21st Century** music.

You can find out about each of classical music's five different stages in the first five chapters of our Incredible Story. By the end of the book, you should be able to work out which one is your favourite.

01
Early Music Period

 For the beginning of our Incredible Story, we are rewinding fourteen hundred years back in time to around the year 600.

It might be a long time ago, but we can work out how music sounded thanks to monks. They used to copy out collections of tunes, which they would then sing in church. Their voices used to echo around the buildings where people came to worship. The sort of music that they sang was called **Gregorian Chant**.

 Hear how **Gregorian Chant** sounds on Track 1 of our online downloads.

Gregorian Chant was named after **Pope Gregory I**. He did not actually invent the music, but he did more or less sort it all out, by getting his people to gather together an official collection of the pieces that were sung at this time. The Pope is the leader of the Catholic Church, so his approval of a piece of music counted for a lot.

INCREDIBLE FACT!

Pope Gregory was in charge of the Catholic Church from around 590 to 604. Other than music, one of his main claims to fame is that he sent Saint Augustine on a mission to England to convert the country to Christianity.

Over the next 400 years, classical music continued to develop with new ideas being introduced by new composers. But basically, most of the sung music that was written sounds similar to **Gregorian Chant**. There was other popular music around back then. But there were no MP3s, CDs or DVDs all that time ago and none of it was written down. So we have no record of what was being played or sung. We can only guess.

INCREDIBLE FACT!

Copying out music was hard work for the monks because they did not use the sort of pens that we use today. Instead, they wrote with feather quills dipped in ink. There were no photocopiers or computer printers, so every piece of music had to be copied out by hand.

 We are fast-forwarding 500 years from the time of **Pope Gregory** to find out about one of the greatest ever female composers.

COMPOSER FILE

NAME: Hildegard of Bingen

BORN: 1098

DIED: 1179

NATIONALITY: German

HER STORY:

Hildegard was born thirty-two years after King Harold of England was killed at the Battle of

Hastings by William the Conqueror's invading army in 1066.

She came from a noble family, but was sent to live in a nunnery when she was just eight years old. She rose up the ranks of the nuns there and thirty years later, she was in charge. About twelve years after that, she set up her own nunnery near the town of Bingen.

She was a very talented woman and was excellent at writing poetry and music. She also became a big thinker in the areas of science and medicine. Hildegard became famous in her lifetime for her dreams. She told everyone who would listen all about them. Many of the influential people of the time travelled from all over Europe to ask for her advice and to listen to her ideas and thoughts.

She set many of her dreams to music and they continue to be performed today.

Hear how Hildegard's music sounds on Track 2 of our online downloads.

We are fast-forwarding by another few hundred years now, past the time when bubonic plague, or the "Black Death", swept across Europe, killing as many

4

as twenty-five million people. This terrible disease was spread by rats. We have also gone past the time in history when Christopher Columbus set sail and discovered the "New World", which we know today as the continents of North and South America.

The Renaissance

We are now in the period of history that we call the **Renaissance**. "Renaissance" is a French word that means "re-birth". It was a time in history when many things changed. There were huge leaps forward in science, in exploring the world, in painting and, of course, in classical music. It is difficult to give an exact date of when the Renaissance in music began, but it was under way by the time that Christopher Columbus was on his voyage across the Atlantic to discover the New World.

> One of Palestrina's most famous pieces was composed around the year 1561. It was dedicated to Pope Marcellus. The Pope only reigned for fifty-five days and never actually heard the music that was written especially for him.
>
> You can hear how it sounds on Track 3 of our online downloads.

The churches and the cathedrals had become bigger by now. And the music had become even more beautiful. **Giovanni da Palestrina** was employed to fill the home of the Catholic Church, the big St Peter's Cathedral in Rome, with amazing music.

Printing

In England, two important things came together to help music move on. Firstly, printing had been invented. Secondly, Queen Elizabeth I came to the throne. Elizabeth liked the new "printing", so she selected two composers, who were called **William Byrd** and **Thomas Tallis**, to be allowed to print music.

Byrd and Tallis are allowed to print music

INCREDIBLE FACT!
The first composer to actually write an opera was an Italian called **Jacopo Peri**. It was called **Dafne**, but is very rarely performed today.

Opera

The next big change in classical music came when composers decided to bring acting together with music, to tell a story through singing. This marks the birth of what we now call "**opera**".

The prize for writing the first important opera usually goes to another Italian. His name was **Claudio Monteverdi** and his opera was called **L'Orfeo**. It told the mythological tale of Orpheus. He was a musician who, when his wife Euridice died, went down to Hades, the land of the dead, to try to get her back. As you will read later in our Incredible Story, it was a tale to which composers would return time and time again.

You can hear how Monteverdi's **L'Orfeo** sounds on Track 4 of our online downloads.

These are the different types of
singer who appear in operas:

Among the men, the **bass** makes
the very lowest sound.

The **baritone** sings a slightly higher part
than the bass; but he has a lower voice than
the tenor.

The **tenor** is probably the most important
male voice in opera. He tends to be given all of
the main romantic roles as well. His voice can
reach higher notes than a baritone's can.

The **countertenor** has the highest of all
men's voices. He sings with a very high-pitched
voice, that you might even mistake for a
woman's!

The **contralto** is the lowest of the female
voices. She can hit many of the same low notes
that a tenor can manage.

The **mezzo-soprano** has a relatively low
woman's voice and is able to reach lower notes
than a soprano.

The **soprano** is probably the most important
female voice in opera. She tends to be paired
up with the tenor for the big romantic lead
roles. She can also hit the highest notes.

02
Baroque Period

 We are leaving the Renaissance Period of classical music behind us now and we are moving into the time that is known as the **Baroque Period**. This lasted for 150 years from 1600 right through until 1750.

How do you say it?

British people say Baroque so that the second half of the word rhymes with "sock". But American people say it differently, with the second half of the word rhyming with "poke".

During the Baroque Period, lots of discoveries were made and theories proved. It must have been a very exciting time to be alive.

The great scientist, Isaac Newton, proved that the earth has a pull of gravity. That is what stops us from floating around like astronauts in a spacecraft. He realised the truth about gravity when an apple fell from a tree and bashed him on the head.

Also around this time, scientists accepted that the earth goes around the sun, instead of believing, as they did before, that the sun went round the earth. That made us much smaller members of the universe.

Previously, people had thought that the earth was the centre of everything.

 We are passing through the time when Guy Fawkes tried to blow up the Houses of Parliament in the Gunpowder Plot; when the Pilgrim Fathers set sail on the *Mayflower* from Plymouth in England for a new life in America; and when King Charles I had his head chopped off.

Our first composer of the Baroque Period is called **Jean-Baptiste Lully**. He worked for King Louis XIV of France as his personal composer. Lully did a lot to change the sound of orchestras at the time and many of his ideas were brand new. He was one of the first people to have an orchestra made up of twenty-four violins and flutes, oboes, bassoons, trumpets and timpani (these are drums).

> 🔊 Hear some of Lully's ballet music on Track 5 of our online downloads.

INCREDIBLE FACT!

Lully used a big stick to conduct his orchestra. He would bang it on the floor in time to the music. One day, he was so excited, conducting one particular piece, that he missed the floor and stabbed his foot with the stick. Medicine was not as good in those days as it is now and poor old Lully died from his injury.

In London, the King of England had a brilliant composer working for him. His name was **Henry Purcell**. He was an amazing young talent and was made Organist of Westminster Abbey when he was just twenty years old. It was one of the biggest jobs in music and was something like being a top pop star today.

Despite the fact that Henry Purcell only lived for another sixteen years, he wrote a huge variety of different types of music, including pieces for King Charles II, King James II and Queen Mary.

He also wrote an opera called **Dido and Aeneas**, which includes one of the most beautiful songs ever written. It is known as **Dido's Lament**. In the story, Dido is the Queen of Carthage. She is in love with Aeneas, who has sailed away to build the city of Rome.

 Dido's Lament is a very sad song because Dido is so lonely. You can hear some of it for yourself on Track 6 of our online downloads.

INCREDIBLE FACT!

The Italian **Tomaso Albinoni** is best known today for one piece, his **Adagio for Organ and Strings**. The trouble is, he didn't write it. Or, at least, he never finished it. An Italian professor found a scrap of manuscript in a German library around two hundred years after Albinoni had died. The professor rebuilt the whole piece around those few lines of music.

The German **Johann Pachelbel** was another composer who was making a name for himself around this time. While he was alive, he was best known for being an organist and writing church music. But today, there is only one piece of his music that is still played often – his **Canon in D**.

 You can hear how it sounds on Track 7 of our online downloads.

This sort of canon has nothing to do with castles or battles. Instead, it is a piece of music with a melody that is played and then imitated by one or more other

instruments. A good example of this is when choirs sing **Frère Jacques**, **London's Burning** or **Three Blind Mice**. Here, the people's voices are the instruments. Pachelbel did exactly the same thing with an orchestra.

INCREDIBLE FACT!

The composer **Arcangelo Corelli** insisted that all the string players in his orchestra played their instruments in exactly the same way – moving their bows up and down in the same direction at the same time. This meant that his orchestras looked and sounded far better than many others at the time.

Our next composer was one of the most famous of all. His name was **Johann Sebastian Bach**.

As well as loving
music, he also
loved to
walk . . .

And walk . . .

And walk . . .

When he was nineteen years old, he made
one particularly long journey. He walked

two hundred and thirteen miles to hear a performance by an organist whom he admired. Once he had heard the concert, he turned around and walked the same distance back home again!

It's probably just as well that Bach enjoyed walking because there were no cars, buses, trains or aeroplanes in those days, so getting about was difficult.

On another of his journeys, this time to the German city of Hamburg, he stayed so long that he nearly ran out of money. He was tired and hungry. As he walked past an inn, the smell of delicious food wafted out. At that moment, he felt even more tired and hungry. He must have looked very sad because somebody inside took pity on him and threw two fishes out of the window. Inside each of them, he found a coin. It meant that he could continue his journey without worrying how he was going to pay for it.

Johann Sebastian Bach was probably the greatest organist to live in the 18th century,

but he never boasted about his achievements. He once said:

There's really nothing remarkable about it. All you have to do is to hit the right key at the right time and the instrument plays itself.

This, of course, is not true. The organ is not an easy instrument to play. Not only do your fingers have to fly over the keys at great speed, but your feet have to press the pedals at the same time . . . without you looking down!

If you want to find how hard that can be, then try using one hand to pat the top of your head, while using your other hand to  rub round and round on your stomach. It is hard, isn't it? Well, it can be just as hard to play the organ with your hands and feet at the same time.

You can hear one of the pieces that Bach composed for the organ on Track 8 of our online downloads.

Bach also loved maths and he liked to play games with numbers in his music. For example, he gave each of the letters of the alphabet a score, depending on its position. So the letter **A** gets **one point**, the letter **B** gets **two points**, the letter **C** gets **three points** and so on, right the way through to the letter **Z**, which gets **twenty-six points**.

B = 2
A = 1
C = 3
H = 8
2+1+3+8 = 14

TRY IT YOURSELF
See what number is important to you by adding up the scores for each of the letters in your name, just like Bach did.

When Bach added up the scores for the letters in his name, he came up with a grand total of fourteen points. Patterns around the number fourteen often appear in his music.

Bach worked as an organist and choirmaster in the German town of Leipzig.

As part of his job, he had to write pieces for the choir to sing to mark major events in the Church calendar. But Bach did not limit himself to music sung in church. He wrote a lot of pieces for orchestra as well. In fact, he composed an incredible amount of music. After he died, it took forty-six years to collect it all together.

Alongside Johann Sebastian Bach, the other really great composer from the Baroque Period was **George Frideric Handel**.

INCREDIBLE FACT!

Handel's father did not approve of his son's love of music. His mother had to smuggle a small keyboard into to the attic of their house. The young boy would play the instrument up there, in secret on his own, when his father was not around.

When Handel was eight years old, a nobleman heard him play the organ in a church and paid for him to have lessons.

But just three years later, when Handel was still only eleven, the teacher admitted that he had taught him everything about music that he could possibly think of.

A few years later, Handel was given a job as a musician by the Elector of Hannover. He was allowed a year's holiday to go to London, where he received offers to write operas. But he stayed longer than he should have done. He was worried about how angry the Elector would be. He wondered about not going back home at all.

Then the Queen of England, Queen Anne, died. She had no children and it was none other than the Elector himself who became the new King of England.

Handel must have been rather nervous when the Elector arrived to be crowned king. But King George I, as the Elector became, forgave Handel for spending so much time away because he was such a brilliant composer.

Handel set about writing a lot of music with a royal theme. In 1717 he composed his

Water Music to be performed on the River Thames. The Royal Family floated along the river on one barge, while the orchestra was crammed onto other barges floating nearby. Luckily, the barges did not sink!

 You can hear the **Hornpipe** from Handel's **Water Music** on Track 9 of our online downloads.

In 1749 King George II asked Handel to write music for a big fireworks concert in Green Park in London. The fireworks were a bit of a letdown. The rockets worked, but the Catherine wheels would not light properly, apart from one. It managed to set fire to a wooden tower that had been especially built for the day. The fire caused a lot of panic, but Handel's **Music for the Royal Fireworks** was a big hit.

Handel wrote incredible music, but he was a very grumpy man. He would often be seen scurrying around the streets of London, muttering to himself. He was also very greedy. Look at what happened once when he was sitting in a restaurant.

Dinner with Handel

23

COMPOSER FILE

NAME: Antonio Vivaldi

BORN: 1678, while an
                 earthquake was going on

DIED: 1741

NATIONALITY: Italian

HIS STORY:

Vivaldi learned a lot about music from his father, who was originally a baker, but became a violinist.

Vivaldi had bright red hair and after he trained to work in the church, he became known as the "Red Priest".

Working as a priest probably did not suit him terribly much and he was always getting into trouble.

Once, right in the middle of a church service, an idea for a brand-new tune came into his head. Instead of waiting until the end of the service to write it down, he stopped in the middle of a sentence and rushed off to scribble down the music, leaving everyone else sitting open mouthed.

Vivaldi claimed that he could not say mass because he suffered from asthma, but that did not stop him from travelling all over Europe conducting his music.

He took with him two singers called Anna and Paolina. Because Vivaldi was a priest, he was not allowed to get married or even to have a

girlfriend. But some people suspected that *both* Anna *and* Paolina were Vivaldi's girlfriends *at the same time!*

He still found time to compose and wrote many operas, hundreds of instrumental pieces and a whole collection of works for choirs to sing.

One of Vivaldi's most famous works is **The Four Seasons**, which sets Spring, Summer, Autumn and Winter to music.

 You can hear part of **Spring** on Track 10 of our online downloads.

03
Classical Period

 We are now out of the Baroque Period and we are into the Classical Period. This runs for about eighty years, roughly from 1750 until 1830.

 Before we carry on, let's just stop for a moment to talk about the Classical Period of classical music. It is easy to become confused when we start talking about music from the Classical Period. Everything that we include in our Incredible Story is classical music, which is different from folk music, pop music, jazz, rock or dance music.

Classical music is usually performed by musicians or singers who do not use microphones or electronic wizardry to create their music. Also, in classical music, the composers are usually more famous than the people who are doing the performing. This is the exact opposite from other types of music, where the performers are the stars and the composers are usually unknown. There are exceptions to both of these rules, but generally they hold true.

BUT . . . As you can see, there is a big "but" because "Classical" also refers to one distinct period of time in our story. One of the big differences between the Classical Period and the Baroque Period is that the Church gradually became less important for composers. Although many of them still wrote religious music, they tended to be employed by royal families or rich noblemen rather than working for churches. Gradually performances in concert halls were becoming more important, too. Until this time, there really were no concert halls as we know them.

This was a time of huge change. And not just in music either. It was a time of scientific invention, too. Steam was used for the first time as a way of powering big machines in factories. James Hargreaves came up with the "Spinning Jenny", a machine that made spinning cotton faster and easier. Britain led the world in the Industrial Revolution, with the number of factories growing fast. This was good news because it meant cheaper clothes and more jobs for everyone. But it was bad news too, because many people – including young children – worked long hours under terrible conditions in dangerous factories.

Things were really starting to change now, not least in the world of opera. As well as people singing on stage, composers such as **Christoph Willibald von Gluck** were including ballet sections in their operas for the first time. Gluck's operas were packed full of new ideas, which created a sound and style that people simply had not heard before.

Some of the composers in our Incredible Story led unhappy lives, but the next one, **Joseph Haydn**, was not one of them. In fact, he was probably one of the most cheerful composers of the whole bunch. He was also one of the most hard working.

During his long life, he wrote more than eighty string quartets and more than fifty piano sonatas. And then there were the twenty operas, as well as many concertos, choral works and chamber music.

What Does It All Mean?

Chamber music – music written for small groups of musicians – the sort of number that you could fit into a room ("chamber") at home

Concerto – a piece for a solo instrument and the whole orchestra, usually divided into three sections, which are known as "movements"

Quartet – a piece of music for four players

Sonata – a piece for a solo instrument, or one instrument and piano, that follows a set of complicated rules

Symphony – a big piece of music for the whole orchestra, usually divided into four fast and slow movements

Movement – a section of a bigger piece of music.

Haydn's biggest achievement of all was his symphonies. They were full of imagination and fun. He wrote one hundred and four of them in total and each one was given a number. His early symphonies tended to start with a fast movement, with a slow movement coming next. And then, they would finish off with another fast movement.

His later symphonies had four different movements. They would start with a fast movement, then would come the slow movement, with *two* fast movements following on.

▶ Number 45 – The Farewell Symphony

Haydn and a group of musicians worked for a rich nobleman. While they were working, they couldn't be with their wives and children. Haydn wanted to remind his boss about this, so the musicians were told to blow out the candles by their music stands one by one and leave the stage. In the end, only the two principal violinists are left.

▶ Number 94 – The Surprise Symphony

Haydn wrote this piece because he wanted to wake up his aristocratic audience in London, who often nodded off when they were listening to a new piece of music after a large meal with lots of wine. First, Haydn lulled them with a quiet bit. And just when they were about to doze off completely . . . the orchestra suddenly

let out a great big **CRASH!** Everybody jumped out of their seats in shock.

You can hear this for yourself on Track 11 of our online downloads.

Number 96 – The Miracle Symphony

This piece is said to have been given this nickname after the audience rushed forward to congratulate Haydn at the end of its first performance. Suddenly, there was a massive crash behind them. A huge chandelier had fallen from the ceiling onto the seats where the people had been sitting just a few moments before. If they had not gathered around Haydn, they would have been seriously hurt. Everybody agreed it was a miracle and the name has stuck ever since.

INCREDIBLE FACT!

The nicknames of some of Haydn's symphonies are **The Schoolmaster, The Clock** and **The Bear**.

Haydn lived to the ripe old age of 77 years. During his lifetime, there were many important developments. Captain Cook, sailing in the South Seas, drew the first proper maps of Australia. English convicts began to be transported to this newly discovered continent. The Americans fought hard against the English and won their independence. France had its violent Revolution and chopped off the heads of its King and Queen. But despite all this happening in the world around him, Haydn still carried on writing his music.

Our next two composers are probably the most incredible of all the composers in our Incredible Story. The first is called **Wolfgang Amadeus Mozart**. He became famous for big orchestral symphonies, for operas, for music sung by choirs, for chamber music and for concertos.

You can hear one of Mozart's most famous pieces, **Eine Kleine Nachtmusik,** which means "A Little Night Music", on Track 12 of our online downloads.

Mozart started playing the keyboard at the age of three and was composing music by the time he was just four years old. He was not the only person in his family to be musically talented. His father, Leopold, was a composer, who worked for the Prince Archbishop of Salzburg in Austria. Wolfgang had a sister called Maria Anna, who was also a good musician. Her family and friends called her by her nickname, Nannerl.

When Leopold realised how musical his children were, he decided to take them on a tour of Europe. Mozart was just six years old.

There was a lot of travelling.

In fact, they travelled for four whole years.

First, they went from Salzburg to Munich, where they both performed concerts.

And then there were concerts in Vienna.

Then it was on to Paris, for more concerts.

And then across the English Channel, to London, for even more concerts.

Then they turned around and went back across the English Channel.

And travelled to Amsterdam, for – yes, that's right – more concerts.

Then it was back on the road again. This time to Munich, where their concert tour had started out.

Finally, four years after they had started, the family returned home to Salzburg. By now, Wolfgang was a star. He had played in front of most of the important people in each of the countries he had visited, including kings and queens.

Mozart Stories

The young Mozart could do all sorts of tricks while sitting at the piano keyboard. One of his favourites was to play with his hands hidden underneath a cloth, so that he could not see any of the keys. His audiences always loved it.

When Mozart was a young boy in Italy, he heard a truly beautiful piece of music called **Miserere**, sung by a choir. It had been written by a famous composer called **Gregorio Allegri**. Mozart loved it so much that apparently he rushed off back to his room and quickly wrote it down. He had heard the piece just twice, but could still remember exactly where all of the notes were supposed to go.

From the age of thirteen, Mozart began working for the Archbishop of Salzburg. Eventually, he annoyed his boss so much that he was sacked from his job. The Archbishop's secretary actually kicked him on the bottom as Mozart left for the final time!

When he was twenty-five years old, Mozart moved to Vienna. He was challenged to a duel, or fight, by another famous composer called **Muzio Clementi**. This was not a duel involving swords or pistols, though. It

was a musical duel, with each man trying to play better than the other on the piano. In the end, the judges decided that each was just as good as the other and declared it a draw.

Some of the music that Mozart wrote was very difficult to play. Once, he even used his nose to hit the notes on the piano that he was unable to reach with his hands.

When Mozart thought of a tune, he just had to write it down. He was never very good at keeping still either. This used to drive his barber mad, because often in the middle of having his hair done, Mozart would suddenly jump up from the seat and charge over to the keyboard because a new idea about a piece of music had burst into his head. The poor old barber would have to chase after him to finish off the job while his customer sat on the piano stool.

Mozart was terrible at looking after his money. During his lifetime, he earned quite a lot, but he spent everything he had and he often borrowed money from his friends.

In the end, he died virtually penniless. It was a sad end for a composer who left behind more than six hundred different pieces of music and was truly excellent at every type of music he tried to write.

The next composer in our Incredible Story might well be the most incredible of them all because he composed some of the most beautiful music ever written, but never actually heard many of his pieces, because he became deaf. His name is **Ludwig van Beethoven**.

COMPOSER FILE

NAME: Ludwig van Beethoven

BORN: 1770

DIED: 1827

NATIONALITY: German

HIS STORY:

Beethoven had a tough childhood. His father was determined that he would be as successful as Mozart and forced him to study the piano all day, every day.

He became a brilliant pianist by the time he was an adult. Audiences flocked to hear him and he

was friends with rich noblemen and noblewomen from Vienna's high society.

By the time he was twenty-six, Beethoven realised he had a problem with his hearing. It gradually became worse and he was completely deaf a few years later. But his deafness never stopped him from composing. It is a sign of how brilliant he was that he carried on, even though he was never able to hear many of his pieces.

He did have trouble coming to terms with losing his hearing, though. During the time he was going deaf, he would angrily thump the piano very hard in an effort to hear the notes, sometimes even breaking the strings of the piano. He must have been very unpopular with his neighbours!

Beethoven was another of those composers who wrote all kinds of music, including concertos, choral works and pieces for solo instruments. His speciality was the symphony, though.

Unlike Mozart, who could dash off his music very quickly, Beethoven tended to spend weeks composing each new work. He ended up writing one of the songs from his opera **Fidelio** no fewer than *eighteen* times.

 You can hear part of one of Beethoven's greatest works, his **Symphony Number 5**, on Track 13 of our online downloads.

Beethoven Stories

Ludwig van Beethoven liked to claim that the "van" in the middle of his name meant that he was related to a royal family, but, in fact, he was descended from a perfectly normal family, with his ancestors originally coming from Holland.

When Beethoven lost his temper, he tended to do it in style. Once, when he was eating in a restaurant, the waiter got in a muddle and brought him a meal that he had not ordered, instead of the one that he wanted. Beethoven was cross. In fact, he was more than cross. He was angry, very angry indeed. He went bright red. He screamed and he shouted. Then he picked up the plate of beef stew in front of him and he threw it at the waiter. The beef stew flew through the air and landed on top of the waiter's head. He had his hands full with other plates. So all the waiter could do was to stand there in the middle of the restaurant with gravy and lumps of meat trickling down his face and the back of his neck.

Beethoven regularly enjoyed eating a soup made from eggs, and whenever his cook served the dish, he always demanded to  inspect the eggs beforehand. If any of them proved to have gone off, he would throw them straight at the poor cook, who would become covered in sticky egg yolk.

Beethoven was incredibly scruffy and not terribly keen on having a bath. So he probably did not smell very sweet either. Once, he was arrested and thrown in prison by a policeman who thought he was a tramp. Despite the scruffy man's shouts of "I am Beethoven!", it took one of the most senior musicians in Vienna to reassure the officer that the tramp was in fact the great composer himself.

Many people believe that Beethoven's **Symphony Number 9** was his biggest triumph. It used a much larger orchestra

than the symphonies written by the composers who had come before him. He even added a big choir and four solo singers. This was revolutionary at the time. When the piece was first performed in public, Beethoven was completely deaf. On the big night, he sat on the stage with his back to the audience. At the end of the concert, it was only when one of the singers turned him around to face the crowd that he realised that they had been wildly cheering and applauding his masterpiece.

INCREDIBLE FACT!

When many musicians look at a page of music, it all comes alive in their heads. So, even though he was deaf, Beethoven could compose the music in his head and write it down on paper. And when he looked at the paper, he could hear the music in his head.

04
Romantic Period

 We are winding the clock forwards again – but not by too many years this time. Earlier in our Incredible Story, we wound on the clock a few hundred years each time. But that is not necessary here. There has been no big jump in time because the composers from the Classical Period had a lot of influence on the composers from the next part of our story, which is known as the **Romantic Period**.

By the end of the Classical Period and the beginning of the Romantic Period, composers were being thought of as stars. They were no longer just servants who were ready to do whatever an aristocrat told them to do. Instead, they began to travel to different countries, earning large amounts of money as performers. Composers had become celebrities in their own right.

The Italian **Niccolò Paganini** was one of those composers who had become a big name around Europe. Audiences crowded into his violin concerts and he was a real showman. If he were alive today, he would be one of those people who would never be out of the newspapers and who would always be appearing on television doing outrageous musical stunts.

He was one of the first concert superstars in music. He would wow audiences by performing all sorts of tricks with his violin. This included playing amazing tunes with just two strings on his violin instead of four. He even deliberately snapped some of the strings in the middle of a performance and still managed to play the piece perfectly.

Much of the music that he wrote was designed to let him show off when he played it in public. At the time, people thought that only Paganini could play such difficult music, but now, more than one hundred and sixty years later, the great young performers of today can play it just as well. But Paganini was famous for being the first to do it.

 You can hear some of his violin music for yourself on Track 14 of our online downloads.

INCREDIBLE FACT!

As well as the violin, Paganini was brilliant at the mandolin, guitar and viola.

The opera composer **Gioachino Rossini** wrote smash hit after smash hit for twenty years. But when he was just thirty-seven years old, he suddenly stopped. During the next thirty years of his life, he composed no opera at all. Nobody is quite sure why he stopped. Perhaps he was rich enough already. Or maybe he was sulking because his final opera, which was called **William Tell**, was not very popular. It is very, very long indeed.

You can hear the overture on Track 15 of our online downloads.

INCREDIBLE FACT!

Composers such as Paganini were able to promote their music around Europe because they were brilliant concert performers. Remember – there was no radio, no television, no internet, no CDs and no MP3s. So, if a composer wanted to show off what he had written, he needed to get it performed regularly in halls packed full of people.

The composer **Franz Schubert** was a one man music factory. Music came so easily to him at any time of the day or night that he could find himself sitting in a café when he would suddenly be struck by a brilliant idea for a piece of music. So he would pick up a pen and write on the café tablecloth or on the back of a menu.

Schubert wrote just over eight and a half symphonies. He wrote the first two movements of his eighth symphony and

then abandoned it. Nobody is quite sure why. It has been given the nickname **The Unfinished** and has become one of his most popular works.

INCREDIBLE FACT!

Schubert wrote more than six hundred songs, which in his language are known as *Lieder*. But despite working hard at his music, he loved a good party with lots of music and fun. These parties were called *Schubertiads* by his friends.

INCREDIBLE FACT!

The Frenchman **Hector Berlioz** learned the flute and the guitar when he was a boy. He grew up to be a very temperamental composer and would fly into a rage at musicians who had not performed his music to the high standard he demanded. His biggest work was the **Requiem**. It was written for an absolutely huge orchestra and choir, as well as four brass bands, one at each corner of the stage.

COMPOSER FILE

NAME: Frédéric Chopin (but his friends called him Fritz)

BORN: 1810

DIED: 1849

NATIONALITY: Polish

HIS STORY:

Chopin is the only composer in the whole of our Incredible Story who is famous for writing for just one instrument.

He loved the piano so much that he wrote no symphonies, no operas and nothing for choirs. During his life, he composed around two hundred pieces of music. One hundred and sixty-nine of them were for solo piano and involved no other instruments at all.

Not only was he one of the greatest composers for piano, he was also a fantastic player. He amazed audiences wherever he went.

He settled down in Paris and lived in quite some style. He paid for his expensive tastes by giving music lessons to rich people in Paris. He never liked the idea of asking them for money, so he would always look away while they left the fee for their lesson on his mantelpiece.

If he were alive today, Chopin would be keen to be seen in the most fashionable clothes with the trendiest designer labels.

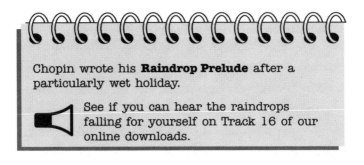

Chopin wrote his **Raindrop Prelude** after a particularly wet holiday.

See if you can hear the raindrops falling for yourself on Track 16 of our online downloads.

The German composer **Felix Mendelssohn** was an incredibly clever child: he was a brilliant painter; he was great at sport; he could speak several languages and he was a very gifted musician.

Mendelssohn gave his first public performance at the piano when he was nine years old. By the time he was sixteen, he had written his **Octet for Strings**. Mendelssohn's family was quite rich and he did not have the same worries about money as some of the other composers in our Incredible Story.

What Does It Mean?

Octet – a piece of music performed by a group of eight musicians

Because he had plenty of money, Mendelssohn travelled a lot, including to Scotland. The weather was very bad while he was there, but his visit still inspired his **Hebrides Overture**, which he wrote about a group of islands in the sea to the very far north of Scotland. He also began writing his **Symphony Number 3** when he was on holiday in Scotland's capital, Edinburgh. This symphony has the nickname **The Scottish**.

INCREDIBLE FACT!

Mendelssohn was one of the first conductors to use a baton to beat time when he stood in front of the orchestra. This helps the players to make sure that they all start and stop at the right time and that they play at the same speed.

Mendelssohn wrote a **Wedding March** for the play, **A Midsummer Night's Dream**. It is still often heard at weddings today.

 You can hear it for yourself on Track 17 of our online downloads.

Once, Mendelssohn was in London with two friends from back home in Germany. They had been out for a very large dinner. As they walked back to their lodgings, Mendelssohn spotted a sign in a butcher's shop window, which said: "German sausages. Two pence each." Even though they were completely full, they could not walk past the shop without sampling some of the food from their homeland. So, each of them bought a sausage and ate it there and then in the street outside. They sang songs as they ate.

Pop stars today have groups of screaming fans following them wherever they go. In his day, the pianist and composer **Franz Liszt** was the closest thing to a pop star. Wherever he went, Liszt was heaped with honours. He counted royalty and aristocracy among his friends.

When Liszt was young, Niccolò Paganini was one of his heroes. This was not just because he was a brilliant musician, but also because he was a real star. When he was still a boy, Liszt decided to become the "Paganini of the Piano". And he succeeded.

His piano pieces are amazingly difficult to play. And he performed them with real pizzazz and style.

Like Paganini, he was mobbed in the street wherever he went, and women fainted with excitement at his concerts.

Romantic Opera

Opera continued to develop throughout the Romantic Period of our Incredible Story.

INCREDIBLE FACT!

The composer **Johannes Brahms** was a master of nearly every type of classical music. He wrote four great symphonies and a lot of chamber music. He was a particularly fine composer of music for the piano, an instrument which he played very well indeed. One of his most popular pieces today is his **Academic Festival Overture**. In it, he included tunes sung by students at the time. At its first performance, when the students heard their college songs in the music, they were so delighted that they stood up, cheered, and threw their hats into the air.

 You can hear part of the **Academic Festival Overture** for yourself on Track 18 of our online downloads.

Richard Wagner from Germany was a brilliant and important composer. But his thoughts and his personality made him a very dislikeable man. He held views about other people that would be completely unacceptable to us today. To get what he wanted, he was prepared to lie, cheat and steal. He would often use people before casting them aside without further

thought. He had a monstrous ego and believed himself to be almost like a god.

Despite his character, he wrote some of the most important and impressive music of the Romantic Period, especially in the world of opera. Generally, his operas are very, very long indeed.

His masterpiece remains the Ring Cycle, which is made up of four different operas, which, if you sang all four of them back to back, would take you more than fifteen hours to complete.

The Ring Cycle is based on Norse mythology and tells stories about gods and heroes ...

... with a sword ...

... a magic helmet that makes the person wearing it disappear ...

... and the all-powerful Ring that carries the curse of a dwarf.

The Valkyries were female goddesses from Norse mythology.

 Listen to how Wagner set to music their ride through the sky on Track 19 of our online downloads.

INCREDIBLE FACT!

The most important Italian composer at this time was **Giuseppe Verdi**. If we translate his name into English, then he would be called Joseph Green. His operas are full of wonderful tunes, such as the **Anvil Chorus**, which is sung by a group of blacksmiths and soldiers in his opera, **Il Trovatore**.

 Hear it for yourself on Track 20 of our online downloads.

While Wagner was writing opera in Germany and Verdi was writing opera in Italy, a man by the name of **Jacques Offenbach** was writing opera in France. He was having great fun and his operas were the talk of the country. He brought a dance called the **Can-Can** to everyone's attention. The important people in Paris pretended to be shocked by lines of ladies kicking their legs high in the air. But secretly, they loved it. Offenbach included the dance in his opera **Orpheus in the Underworld**.

Both the dance and the opera itself became a smash hit. You can hear why on Track 21 of our online downloads.

Although our next composer, **Georges Bizet**, was also French, he became famous for **Carmen**, an opera that was set in Spain. Through his music, he was able to conjure up the sounds of Spain, where bullfighting with brave matadors wearing bright red capes were a common sight.

Poor old Bizet died before everyone realised just how brilliant **Carmen** really was. Bizet apparently said that the first performance was "a definite and hopeless flop". But just a few years later, it was an enormous success and was being performed in all of the major cities across Europe.

Shall We Dance?

You might think that with all this talk about opera, singing was the only thing going on during this part of our Incredible Story. But you would be wrong, because in Vienna in Austria, dancing was all the fashion – in particular, waltzing.

When the waltz first appeared, it was seen as being scandalous, because the men and women danced face to face very closely to one another. But then it became popular in the most elegant salons.

The women wore long dresses and the men were dressed in smart dinner jackets, and the rooms were filled with glittering

chandeliers and the glasses overflowed with sparkling champagne.

Johann Strauss was known as "the Father of the Waltz". He wrote more than two hundred waltzes in total. But it was his son, confusingly also called **Johann Strauss**, who had the greatest success with them.

He set up a rival orchestra to his father's and composed four hundred waltzes, as well as three hundred other dances. These included polkas, galops and marches. Johann Senior may have been known as "the Father of the Waltz", but Johann Junior eventually became known as "the Waltz King".

His waltzes went down a storm both in the Viennese cafés and on his many tours across Europe and to the United States. He made a fortune from the waltz, but then he did compose the most famous of them all: **The Blue Danube**.

 You can hear it on Track 22 of our online downloads.

INCREDIBLE FACT!

The most popular drink in the coffee houses of Vienna is coffee with mountains of whipped cream on top. It goes well with the waltzes and if you go to Vienna today, you will still hear **The Blue Danube** as you drink your coffee with whipped cream.

The next composer in our Incredible Story was a real brain-box when he was a boy. His name is **Camille Saint-Saëns** and he was born in Paris in 1835. He was incredibly clever:

Aged 2 . . . he could read and write words.
Aged 3 . . . he was starting to write tunes on the piano.
Aged 5 . . . he gave his first piano concert.
Aged 7 . . . he was an expert in the study of butterflies.
Aged 10 . . . he could play any of Beethoven's 32 piano sonatas from memory.

His best known work is **The Carnival of the Animals**. It was never performed in his lifetime, because he was afraid that once people had heard it, they would no longer see him as a serious composer.

In the carnival, there was the big, slow elephant with its big ears flapping in the wind.

You can hear the elephant's music on Track 23 of our online downloads.

Following on behind the elephant, there were some fossils, with skeleton bones rattling together.

And then came the beautiful, graceful swan, swimming along with its long, white neck held high.

At the same time that **Saint-Saëns** was making a name for himself in Paris, another French composer was doing the same thing just across the city. His name was **Léo Delibes**. He was excellent at writing music for ballet. His most

famous is **Coppélia**, which tells the story of a doll that comes to life.

 You can hear it for yourself on Track 24 of our online downloads.

We have not visited Russia so far in our Incredible Story. Russia is a massive country, full of big differences. Some parts are covered in snow, while others are almost like deserts.

Russian composers during the Romantic Period were keen to find their own style that made them sound different from composers in other countries. Five of them formed a group that was known in Russia as **The Mighty Handful**. They wanted to make their music sound very Russian.

The Mighty Handful

The three most famous members of this group were **Alexander Borodin**, **Modest Mussorgsky** and **Nikolai Rimsky-Korsakov**.

Alexander Borodin did not actually start out as a composer. He trained as a scientist, ending up as a professor, so the first things that he had printed were not musical at all. They were scientific research papers. He is remembered now for two musical works: his opera **Prince Igor** and an orchestral piece called **In the Steppes of Central Asia**.

Modest Mussorgsky wrote the first truly great piano work by a Russian composer. His first job was in the army, but eventually music took over. His piano piece **Pictures at an Exhibition** describes the composer walking through an art gallery, looking at the paintings produced by a close friend.

Nikolai Rimsky-Korsakov was another composer who started out with a different job. He was in the navy. Eventually, he became a music professor, but he taught himself most of what he knew on the subject. He once admitted that what he learned one day he would have to teach to his students the next.

Imagine having a teacher who was only two pages ahead of you in the textbook!

Rimsky-Korsakov's greatest work was **Scheherezade**, which is based on a series of ancient stories. The stories lasted for a thousand and one nights. Of course, there was no television or radio back then, so storytelling was a major part of life. But even so, a thousand and one nights is a very long time – nearly three whole years!

 You can hear part of it on Track 25 of our online downloads.

Pyotr Ilyich Tchaikovsky was also Russian, but he was not a member of the group of composers who called themselves The Mighty Handful. His symphonies, piano concertos and ballets are packed full of wonderful tunes.

 Tchaikovsky's Most Famous Ballets

Sleeping Beauty tells the story of Princess Aurora, who falls into a deep sleep after pricking her finger. She sleeps for a hundred years until a passing prince kisses her. She wakes up and they get married.

Swan Lake tells the story of Odette, the Swan Queen. She has been turned into a swan by an evil sorcerer. In this story, the handsome prince is very nearly tricked into marrying the sorcerer's daughter, rather than Odette. In the end, their love wins through and the evil spell is broken. Odette permanently turns back into her human form and she lives happily ever after with her prince.

 You can hear part of **Swan Lake** on Track 26 of our online downloads.

The Nutcracker tells the story of a girl who is given a nutcracker for Christmas. That night, it comes to life and turns into a prince. The girl is whisked off to the Land of Sweets. There, they meet the Sugar Plum Fairy and there is lots of dancing and fun. The next morning, everything is back to normal and the girl wakes up at home under the Christmas tree.

 Tchaikovsky's biggest triumph was the **1812 Overture**. It was written to celebrate Napoleon's defeat in Russia in that year. It is now very popular at outdoor concerts during the summer, with fireworks adding to the cannon that boom out towards the end.

Tchaikovsky needed help paying the bills. Luckily for him, a rich widow, called Madame Nadezhda von Meck, gave him money to write music. There was one rule that he had to follow if he wanted to continue to receive her money. She had always said that the two of them should never meet. If they ever did, they were to completely ignore each other. It was a strange request, but Tchaikovsky needed the money, so he agreed to it.

Antonín Dvořák loved the folk tunes of his Czech homeland. His father used to play the violin at weddings and, when he was a boy, Dvořák would accompany him on the zither. A zither looks like a funny shaped guitar; it is not used much in classical music these days.

Dvořák's childhood was filled with the music that was played by local peasants. These cheerful folkdances had been handed down from generation to generation. He loved the simple tunes that he heard in the inns and in the village squares and these stayed with him right through his life.

INCREDIBLE FACT!

Dvořák was a train spotter. In fact, he was more than just a train spotter. He was absolutely mad about trains and everything to do with them! When he became a teacher, he would always ask his pupils to describe in detail any train journeys that they had recently made. He would listen to their stories with his complete attention.

When Dvořák was given an important job in America, it was difficult for him to continue with his hobby of train spotting, because only passengers were allowed on the platforms at the station in New York. But then he discovered a new passion. This time it was for steamships. He would make regular journeys to New York's harbour to inspect the big passenger ships that had docked there.

He enjoyed looking after pigeons and, when he was in America, he loved visiting the aviary, where they kept the birds, in the middle of the zoo in New York's Central Park. He was an expert in the various different breeds of pigeon and would visit the zoo as often as he could to look at the

birds. Once Dvořák became interested in something, he *really* became interested in it!

 Dvořák fell in love with the music he heard while he was in America. He wrote his **Symphony Number 9**, which became known as **The New World Symphony**, after listening to African American spirituals, although the tunes that Dvořák wrote were all his own.

 You can hear one of the most famous parts of the symphony on Track 27 of our online downloads.

It was quite a few pages ago in our Incredible Story that we were last in England. In fact, it was way back when Handel was writing music for King George II.

Queen Victoria was on the throne when the English composer **Arthur Sullivan** began working with W.S. Gilbert. Together, they wrote **operettas**. These are like operas, but are more light-hearted and fun. In Gilbert and Sullivan's case, Gilbert wrote the words and Sullivan wrote the music.

They had a very successful partnership, but the two men did not get on terribly well. They would have enormous arguments about little things. One of their biggest bust-ups was about a new carpet at the Savoy Theatre in London, where their operettas were staged.

Gilbert and Sullivan's thirteen operettas included **H.M.S. Pinafore**, which gently made fun of the Royal Navy, and **The Pirates of Penzance**, which teased people in positions of power in Britain at the time. A good example of this was the Modern Major General, who appears in the operetta. He was an expert on absolutely everything except for being in charge of an army – the job that he was supposed to be able to do!

INCREDIBLE FACT!

In Gilbert and Sullivan's operetta **The Grand Duke,** there are two songs all about eating sausage rolls!

69

We are back in France now for the next stage of our Incredible Story. Towards the end of the 19th century, we find the composer **Claude Debussy** busy trying out brand new ideas in classical music. He was known as an **Impressionist** composer.

But this was not because he was doing an impression of anyone else. It was because he broke the rules that people then believed composers should follow.

The same thing happened with a group of painters who were around at the same time. The painters, such as Claude Monet, were also French and were also known as **Impressionists**.

The painters and the musicians wanted to give a general impression of moods and feelings in a much freer way, rather than presenting an exact copy of what they saw.

 Another French Impressionist composer, **Maurice Ravel**, is most famous today for his **Boléro**. It was chosen by the skaters Jayne Torvill and Christopher

Dean as the piece of music for their gold medal-winning ice dance at the Olympic Games in 1984.

 You can hear the music for yourself on Track 28 of our online downloads.

INCREDIBLE FACT!

When he was a boy, the Spanish composer **Isaac Albéniz** used to perform an extraordinary musical trick on the piano to earn money. He would stand with the keyboard behind him and would play tunes with his hands behind his back. It is incredibly difficult to do. You should try it yourself next time you are walking past a piano. Just to add to the show, Albéniz did it dressed as a musketeer. There is no need for you to try that though, unless you really want to!

 By the 1880s, there had been huge changes in people's lives. There was gas lighting on the streets of the big cities. That made them a lot safer because people walking could see where they were going. The roads had improved too; and so had the standard of health.

Cities were getting bigger all over Europe. In the United States of America,

the Civil War was over, and slavery had been abolished. Trains were now criss-crossing Europe, which made long journeys in horse-drawn carriages a thing of the past. Steel ships powered by steam engines were transforming travel by boat.

The world was really changing – and so was music.

COMPOSER FILE

NAME:	Edward Elgar
BORN:	1857
DIED:	1934
NATIONALITY:	English
HIS STORY:	

Elgar's father ran a music shop in Worcester and was an organist at the local church. As a boy, young Edward learned to play the organ. By the time he was twelve years old, he was standing in for his father as church organist.

When he was sixteen years old, he made money by giving violin and piano lessons, as well as playing the violin in local orchestras and doing some conducting.

He had to work hard to make it as a composer and it was a piece called the **Enigma Variations**

that made him famous. This was a series of musical pictures of his friends, his wife and himself.

So, rather than an actual picture of them, he wrote a tune that reminded him of them. One of his friends seemed sad; another hurried about; and one chattered a lot. You can hear this in each of the tunes that Elgar wrote about them.

Elgar's music was very English and his **Pomp and Circumstance March Number 1** is often performed. You might know it better by the words that we sing to one of its tunes: **Land of Hope and Glory**.

 You can hear part of it on Track 29 of our online downloads.

INCREDIBLE FACT!

The English composer Edward Elgar and the Italian composer Giacomo Puccini both had big bushy moustaches.

See for yourself:

Elgar   Puccini

In Italy, **Giacomo Puccini** had taken over from Giuseppe Verdi as the Italian king of opera. Puccini composed a series of extremely popular operas including one called **Turandot**. It includes one of the most famous arias ever written: **Nessun Dorma**. This translates from the Italian as "None Shall Sleep". You might have heard it being sung at football matches, where it has become very popular over the past few years, thanks to a group of singers called The Three Tenors.

 You can hear **Nessun Dorma** on Track 30 of our online downloads.

INCREDIBLE FACT!

The Austrian composer **Gustav Mahler** discovered a piano in his grandmother's attic when he was six years old. Just four years later, he gave his first public performance. He went on to be one of the greatest composers of symphonies in the whole of the Romantic Period of classical music.

INCREDIBLE FACT!

The composer **Paul Dukas** is famous for just one big hit – and he has Mickey Mouse to thank for that. When Walt Disney decided to make a cartoon film starring Mickey with a classical music soundtrack, one of the pieces that he chose was written by the Frenchman. The film was called **Fantasia** and the piece was **The Sorcerer's Apprentice**.

 Hear for yourself on Track 31 of our online downloads.

The prize for the strangest composer in the whole of our Incredible Story must go to the French composer **Erik Satie**.
He gave his music the weirdest titles. What do you think of these?

> Five Grins or Mona Lisa's Moustache
> Three Pieces in the Shape of a Pear
> The Waltz of the Chocolate Almonds
> Things Seen From the Left and Right
>   Without Spectacles
> Veritable Flabby Preludes (for a Dog)

Satie also wrote one of the longest pieces of music in our story. It was for piano and had one hundred and eighty notes, which had to be repeated eight hundred and forty

75

times. When it was presented in New York in 1963, five different pianists had to play in relays all night long to give it a full performance.

 Satie did write some more normal pieces too, as you can hear on Track 32 of our online downloads.

Towards the end of the 19th century, composers were still writing pieces for large orchestras. One of the best examples of this was **Richard Strauss**, who was born in Germany in 1864. He was no relation to the famous waltzing Strauss family from Vienna. We heard about them earlier in our Incredible Story. Richard Strauss's music was quite a bit more serious and he wrote a lot of operas and songs.

 You can hear one of his most famous pieces on Track 33 of our online downloads.

Our next composer put his home country of Finland on the musical map in such a big way that the Finnish government even wanted to put up a statue of him while he was still alive. But the modest composer persuaded them not to. His name was **Jean Sibelius**. The people of Finland loved him. Sibelius's music is very heavily influenced by Finnish legends and history. His most popular piece of music even has the title **Finlandia**.

You can hear part of it on Track 34 of our online downloads.

INCREDIBLE FACT!

Sibelius was actually given the first name **Johan** when he was born. That is the Finnish version of the English name **John**. But when he found out that his uncle had turned his name into **Jean**, which is the French version of **John**, Sibelius decided to do the same thing.

As you may have noticed, many composers used the folksongs of their country in their music. The English composer, **Ralph Vaughan Williams** was no exception.

He composed music for all sorts of instruments, including the mighty brass tuba and the harmonica (or mouth organ).

Vaughan Williams is best known today for a piece where the violin plays the part of one of the beautiful larks that he would have heard while he travelled across the English countryside, collecting folk tunes. It is called **The Lark Ascending**.

You can hear part of it on Track 35 of our online downloads.

INCREDIBLE FACT!

Vaughan Williams's first name **Ralph** is pronounced "Rafe" to rhyme with "safe" and not "Ralph" to rhyme with "Alf".

Vaughan Williams studied at the Royal College of Music in London, at the same time as another English composer, **Gustav Holst**. When he left college, Holst earned his living as a trombonist, before becoming a teacher. Although he wrote lots of other music, his most famous music by far is **The Planets Suite**.

Each movement tells the story of the characters of each of the planets. There are only seven movements because Pluto hadn't been discovered yet (though some people now say Pluto isn't a planet!) and Holst didn't write a movement for Earth. The movements are:

Mars, the bringer of war
Venus, the bringer of peace
Mercury, the winged messenger of the gods
Jupiter, the bringer of jollity
Saturn, the bringer of old age
Uranus, the magician
Neptune, the mystic

You can hear Holst's **Jupiter** on Track 36 of our online downloads.

The Russian composer **Sergei Rachmaninov** was not world famous for just one musical skill or even for just two musical skills. He was famous for three completely different skills: he was a magnificent composer; he was an awesome conductor; and he was a superb pianist.

Rachmaninov lived for seventy years, right through the First World War and halfway through the Second World War. During his

life, horses and carriages were replaced by cars as the way in which everyone travelled around. People started to have telephones in their homes. And everyone listened to music and news on their radios. So, the sort of world that Rachmaninov lived in was much more like the world we know today than it was for any of the other composers whom we have met so far in our Incredible Story.

INCREDIBLE FACT!

When he was a boy, everyone realised that Rachmaninov had a talent for making music, so he went to study at the Saint Petersburg Conservatory. This is not the sort of conservatory that you have attached to your house, where you might eat breakfast when it is particularly sunny. This sort of conservatory is another name for a special music school. It comes from the French word *conservatoire*. Rachmaninov went on to study at the Moscow Conservatory as well as the one in Saint Petersburg.

When he was at the Moscow Conservatory, Rachmaninov played in front of the great Russian composer, Pyotr Ilyich Tchaikovsky. Tchaikovsky was amazed by

Rachmaninov's performing and composing. He gave him the highest marks that had ever been awarded in the conservatory's history.

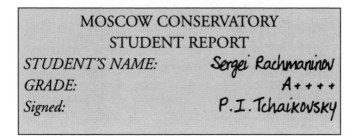

MOSCOW CONSERVATORY
STUDENT REPORT

STUDENT'S NAME: Sergei Rachmaninov

GRADE: A + + + +

Signed: P.I.Tchaikovsky

Rachmaninov was not always so popular with people who listened to his music, though. Audiences and critics in Russia hated his **First Symphony** when they first heard it. He was very hurt and tore his copy of the music into little pieces.

After that, he found it hard to write anything at all. In the end, he went to see Doctor Nikolai Dahl, who managed to help him feel better about writing music.

Once he was completely better, he wrote a masterpiece, his **Second Piano Concerto**. It became the single most popular piece of music that he ever wrote.

You can hear part of it on Track 37 of our online downloads.

INCREDIBLE FACT!

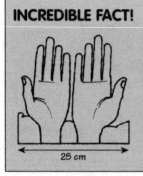

25 cm

Rachmaninov had an enormous pair of hands! It meant that he could play a really wide range of notes on the piano.

Towards the end of his life, Rachmaninov went to live in the American city of Los Angeles. He built himself a new home that was absolutely identical to the one he had left behind in Moscow. He became an American citizen and drove a large Cadillac. He was incredibly proud of that car!

05

20th and 21st Century Period

 We are now at the beginning of the 20th century, just over one hundred years ago. Music started to change again. Romantic composers began to make way for more modern composers.

When the audience heard the music to **Igor Stravinsky's** ballet **The Rite of Spring**, there was a riot. Fighting broke out between those people who did not like the sound of his new style of music and those people who did.

Another Russian composer, **Sergei Prokofiev**, also wrote ballet music. His ballets include **Romeo and**

Juliet, which tells the story of a boy and a girl from two warring families, who fall in love.

 You can hear one of the most famous parts of the ballet on Track 38 of our online downloads.

Prokofiev also wrote a musical tale for children, called **Peter and the Wolf**. It is for a storyteller, accompanied by the whole orchestra. Prokofiev decided to give characters to some of the instruments: the clarinet is a cat, the flute is a bird, the bassoon is Peter's grumbling grandfather, and Peter himself is played by the whole string section.

In 1904, two men sat in a Budapest coffee house, having a conversation that would change their lives. Their names were **Béla Bartók** and **Zoltán Kodály**. They decided to travel around their homeland, away from the cities and into the countryside, with a very early recording machine. They collected folk tunes sung by local countrymen and women. This was one of the first times that someone had tried to save traditional folksongs which were being forgotten. But, thanks to Bartók and Kodály, many Hungarian folksongs are still remembered today.

Some of the modern composers who eventually did new things in music started off by writing pieces that were still Romantic in style. One of those is **Arnold Schoenberg**. He began by writing music that sounded like the late 19th century tunes. But, after a while, he came up with some new ideas about the way that classical music should be written.

Rather than thinking of a tune, composers such as Schoenberg organised music differently, building patterns with the notes that were often based on groups of numbers. His music came to sound very different from what everyone had been used to.

Schoenberg taught two other composers, **Anton Webern** and **Alban Berg**, about his new way of thinking and they took this style of music even further away from the big, beautiful Romantic sound that had made Rachmaninov famous.

Music was very important in the United States of America, but it has a rather different history from the rest of the world. All through the 18th and 19th centuries, people came to live in America, the "New World", from parts of the "Old World".

As the 20th century got going, ragtime, blues, jazz, musicals and pop music became very important. Everyone was tapping their feet to different kinds of rhythms. American classical music began to reflect this.

You can hear this for yourself on Track 39 of our online downloads, with music by the American composer **George Gershwin**. He was one of the richest composers in the whole of our Incredible Story, earning a fortune from his music.

Aaron Copland was born in America, but went off to study in Paris because his parents felt it was the best place for their very talented son to learn about music. When he came back to America, he had found a way of giving his music a very American sound.

Copland wrote ballets with a real American theme, including **Appalachian Spring**, **Billy the Kid** and **Rodeo**.

INCREDIBLE FACT!

Copland's best-known work is called **Fanfare for the Common Man**. It is used now at American presidential inaugurations, the ceremony where somebody officially becomes the next president of the United States.

 You can hear it for yourself on Track 40 of our online downloads.

One of the best-loved pieces of American classical music was composed by **Samuel Barber**. He had a good singing voice and actually recorded himself performing some of his own work. But his real hit was called **Adagio for Strings**.

You can hear it for yourself on Track 41 of our online downloads. First of all, Samuel Barber wrote **Adagio for Strings** for a string quartet. Later, he built it up into a piece for full string orchestra. And then he arranged it again, this time for a choir to sing.

Leonard Bernstein was another great American composer. He became famous for writing successful Broadway musicals. He was also a superb conductor and a brilliant pianist. He was the first composer to become a television and radio star and he also hosted young people's concerts for much of his life.

His most popular work is called **West Side Story**. It is an up-to-date version of William Shakespeare's **Romeo and Juliet**. It started life as a very successful musical in 1957. Bernstein later turned the main tunes into a suite to be played by an orchestra. It even became a popular film.

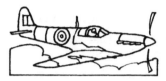 You can hear part of **West Side Story** on Track 42 of our online downloads.

By now, in our Incredible Story, films and the cinema are becoming more important.

William Walton wrote a lot of music for films. He was born in Oldham in 1902 and he became one of the most important English composers in the years between the First and Second World Wars. His film music includes the **Spitfire Prelude and Fugue** from a movie about the Royal Air Force.

You can hear it on Track 43 of our online downloads.

INCREDIBLE FACT!

 William Walton also wrote music for royal occasions, including **Crown Imperial** for the coronation of King George V and **Orb and Sceptre** for the coronation of Queen Elizabeth II.

William Walton was one of the greatest English composers between the two world wars, but **Benjamin Britten** is seen as being the greatest English composer since the end of the Second World War.

He lived in Aldeburgh in Suffolk, where he founded the music festival that still runs every year.

As well as opera, choral music, orchestral works and songs, he also wrote **The Young Person's Guide to the Orchestra**. It uses a tune by the English composer Henry Purcell. You might remember him from quite a few pages ago. He was once a top organist at Westminster Abbey. If you want to listen to more classical music after you have finished reading our Incredible Story, then **The Young Person's Guide to the Orchestra** is a great place to start.

 You can hear some of it on Track 44 of our online downloads.

The Russian composer, **Dmitri Shostakovich**, was another composer who wrote music for films. He also wrote two

Jazz Suites. But Shostakovich's music was not generally light and frothy. He lived in difficult times in the Soviet Union. This was a Communist country in which composers had to follow the rules. Shostakovich broke these rules and got into trouble.

INCREDIBLE FACT!

One of Shostakovich's songs was sung by the cosmonaut Yuri Gagarin over the radio from his spacecraft to Mission Control down on earth.

Our Incredible Story has now arrived at a time when classical music split into two different types. The first involved quite traditional styles, with nice melodies. This was the sort of music that Vaughan Williams and Rachmaninov had written. The second path involved more adventurous, experimental music. This was

more like the music of Schoenberg and Webern. It is known as *avant-garde* music.

The American composer **John Cage** attempted to push the boundaries of what it is that we actually call "music". He even wrote a piece for twelve radios.

John Cage's piece called **4'33"** was the first ever piece of classical music without any notes, as you can see on the next page.

INCREDIBLE FACT!

John Cage created a very different sound with an instrument he called a **prepared piano**. He put bits of rubber, wood and stone between the strings of the piano. It was like nothing that anyone had heard before!

The American composers **Steve Reich** and **Philip Glass** have become famous for writing a type of music called **minimalism**. In this style of music, the composer repeats the same notes over and over again, changing only small details as he goes. It feels a bit like being on a train, where you have the regular clatter of the wheels, but the landscape is changing as you go past it.

The pianist walks onto the stage ...

... sits down at the piano ... and makes no sound at all.

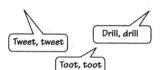

Tweet, tweet

Drill, drill

Toot, toot

The audience listens to whatever sounds are happening in the background.

This, ladies and gentlemen, is my latest piece of music.

A performance of John Cage's piece with no notes

If you are travelling through the countryside, it all looks the same for a while, but then it changes when you go through a city. And everything looks the same there for a while too. Minimalism in music is just like that.

 Hear how Philip Glass's music sounds for yourself on Track 45 of our online downloads.

Today, composers are still writing music to be played by orchestras, by small groups of musicians and by solo performers. New operas and ballets are also being performed right around the world.

Singing is just as popular as it has ever been. Some of the most popular composers who are alive today became famous for the pieces that they have written for choirs to sing.

The Welsh composer **Karl Jenkins** and the English composer **Howard Goodall** have both become famous for writing choral music. You often hear many of their tunes on the television and the radio.

 You can hear their music on Tracks 46 and 47 of our online downloads.

Through the years, composers have often written music to accompany plays in theatres. This is known as **incidental music**. When the cinema first became popular there was no sound, so composers started writing music to accompany the pictures on the screen.

A few years later, when sound was added, composers still wrote music to be used in the films.

Some of the most successful and famous classical composers today are best known for their film music. This film music is often played in concert halls by big orchestras, as well as being heard in cinemas and on DVDs.

 95

The American **John Williams** is probably the world's most famous film composer. He has written music for films including **Harry Potter**, **Superman** and **ET**.

Hear part of **Hedwig's Theme** from **Harry Potter** on Track 48 of our online downloads.

The Canadian **Howard Shore** has composed the music for all three of **The Lord of the Rings** films.

Hear part of it for yourself on Track 49 of our online downloads.

Hans Zimmer originally came from Germany, but now lives in America. His most famous film music is for **Gladiator**.

Hear for yourself on Track 50 of our online downloads.

The Future

That is the Incredible Story of classical music . . . so far. Our journey may have lasted for more than fourteen hundred years, starting at the time of Gregorian Chant. But it does not really end here, because composers all over the world are still writing classical music today. So, music will go on changing as composers introduce new ideas over the decades and centuries ahead.

We know that without music, singing and instruments, the world would be a quieter place. But don't you think it would be a far, far less interesting place too?

97

06

Have a Listen For Yourself!

We have got together with iTunes to bring you a special playlist of all of the different tracks that we have highlighted during our Incredible Story. To hear free samples of each of the pieces and to find out how you can buy them as downloads to your iPod or computer, go online to www.classicfm.com/incredible

Here are the details for all fifty of the tracks:

Track 1: Anonymous
Gregorian chant from the *Proper of the Mass: Introitus – Adorate Deum*

Track 2: Hildegard of Bingen
O Ignis Spiritus

Track 3: Giovanni Pierluigi da Palestrina
Missa Papae Marcelli

Track 4: Claudio Monteverdi
"Ecco pir ch'a voi" from *L'Orfeo*

Track 5: Jean-Baptiste Lully
Entrée from *Ballet des Plaisirs*

Track 6: Henry Purcell
Dido's Lament from *Dido and Aeneas*

Track 7: Johann Pachelbel
Canon in D

Track 8: Johann Sebastian Bach
Toccata and Fugue in D minor

Track 9: George Frideric Handel
Alla Hornpipe from *Water Music*

Track 10: Antonio Vivaldi
Spring from *The Four Seasons*

Track 11: Franz Joseph Haydn
Symphony No. 94 "The Surprise"

Track 12: Wolfgang Amadeus Mozart
Eine Kleine Nachtmusik

Track 13: Ludwig van Beethoven
Symphony No. 5

Track 14: Niccolò Paganini
Caprice No. 24 in A minor

Track 15: Gioachino Rossini
Overture to *William Tell*

Track 16: Frédéric Chopin
Prelude in D Flat "Raindrop"

Track 17: Felix Mendelssohn
Wedding March from *A Midsummer Night's Dream*

Track 18: Johannes Brahms
Academic Festival Overture

Track 19: Richard Wagner
The Ride of the Valkyries

Track 20: Giuseppe Verdi
Anvil Chorus from *Il Trovatore*

Track 21: Jacques Offenbach
Can-Can from *Orpheus in the Underworld*

Track 22: Johann Strauss II
By the Beautiful Blue Danube

Track 23: Camille Saint-Saëns
The Carnival of the Animals

Track 24: Léo Delibes
Coppélia

Track 25: Nikolai Rimsky-Korsakov
Scheherazade

Track 26: Pyotr Ilyich Tchaikovsky
Swan Lake

Track 27: Antonín Dvořák
Symphony No. 9 "From the New World"

Track 28: Maurice Ravel
Boléro

Track 29: Edward Elgar
Pomp and Circumstance March No. 1

Track 30: Giacomo Puccini
Nessun Dorma from *Turandot*

Track 31: Paul Dukas
The Sorcerer's Apprentice

Track 32: Erik Satie
Gymnopédie No. 1

Track 33: Richard Strauss
Also Sprach Zarathustra

Track 34: Jean Sibelius
Finlandia

Track 35: Ralph Vaughan Williams
The Lark Ascending

Track 36: Gustav Holst
Jupiter from *The Planets Suite*

Track 37: Sergei Rachmaninov
Piano Concerto No. 2

Track 38: Sergei Prokofiev
Dance of the Knights from *Romeo and Juliet*

Track 39: George Gershwin
Rhapsody in Blue

Track 40: Aaron Copland
Fanfare for the Common Man

Track 41: Samuel Barber
Adagio for Strings

Track 42: Leonard Bernstein
West Side Story Suite

Track 43: William Walton
Spitfire Prelude and Fugue

Track 44: Benjamin Britten
The Young Person's Guide to the Orchestra

Track 45: Philip Glass
Violin Concerto

Track 46: Karl Jenkins
Benedictus from *The Armed Man (A Mass for Peace)*

Track 47: Howard Goodall
The Lord's My Shepherd

Track 48: John Williams
Hedwig's Theme from *Harry Potter*

Track 49: Howard Shore
The Fellowship of the Ring from *Lord of the Rings*

Track 50: Hans Zimmer
Gladiator Suite

07

Where to Find Out More

Radio

 Now that you have read our Incredible Story, we hope that you will want to find out even more about the amazing world of classical music. One of the best ways to discover what you like about classical music is to tune into Classic FM. We broadcast 24 hours a day across the UK on 100–102 FM and also on DAB Digital Radio and through digital satellite and cable television. You can also listen online at www.classicfm.com. We play all the different types of classical music described in this book and listening to us is a great way to discover new favourites for yourself.

Online

As well as being able to listen to the radio station at www.classicfm.com, you will also find loads of stories, audio clips and pictures that will help you to learn more about classical music in our Learning Zone.

Books and audiobooks

If you would like to discover more about classical composers and the music that they have written over the years, then you might enjoy three audiobooks published by Naxos Audiobooks and Classic FM. This book is based on the first of these, *The Story of Classical Music*, which includes more than one hundred and fifty musical excerpts. The second and third audiobooks in the series, *Famous Composers* and *More Famous Composers*, take the lives of six composers and explore them in more detail. We also recommend the excellent book *Meet the Instruments of the Orchestra!* by Genevieve Helsby (published by Naxos Books). With lots of colour pictures, it will help you to become a real expert in the different

instruments that come together to make an orchestra.

Magazines

 For the latest details of new classical CD and download releases and for the latest news on everything that is happening in the world of classical music, try reading *Classic FM Magazine*, which is published every month and is available from most large newsagents. It comes with at least one free CD attached each month, so you can start to build up your own collection of classical music.

On CD

 If you look in the classical section of any music store, you will find that there are thousands of different recordings of classical music available. It can be a bit confusing to try to work out which one is which. At Classic FM, we've teamed up with HMV and the UK's largest classical music record company, Universal Music, to create a range of top-quality full-length recordings of the most popular classical pieces. The series is called *The Classic FM Full Works* and we are adding new releases all the time. You can find them in HMV stores or online at hmv.co.uk. We've been very careful to choose the highest quality recordings and you will find that none of the CDs is too expensive, so you should be able to afford to build up your collection more quickly.

Live music

The very best way of finding out more about which pieces of classical music you like is by going out and hearing a live performance for yourself. There is

nothing better than hearing an orchestra playing right in front of you. Classic FM works very closely with a group of orchestras across the country: the Royal Scottish National Orchestra, the Royal Liverpool Philharmonic Orchestra, the Philharmonia Orchestra, the Northern

Sinfonia and the London Symphony Orchestra. All of them put on special concerts and events for people who are at school. To see if they have a concert coming up somewhere near you, log on to www.classicfm.com and click on the "Concerts and Events" section.

Thank You

Although the author has his name on the front cover, writing a book like this involves a lot of different people. First of all, a very big thank you to Nicolas Soames and Genevieve Helsby for allowing me to use material from the Naxos Audiobook *The Story of Classical Music* in this new book.

Writers might come up with the words, but without publishers, books would never actually happen. So, thank you to Katie Roden and Ginny Catmur at Hodder Education for working so quickly to turn the words I wrote on my computer into the book that you are holding now.

At Classic FM, I am really grateful to Tim Lihoreau, Sam Jackson, Stuart Campbell, Emma Oxborrow, Charlotte Rosier, Giles Pearman, Vicki Simpson and Rupert Reid for all the advice they have given me.

Finally, the biggest thank you of all goes to Rick Wills, Manon Williams, Rebecca Eastmond and Stephanie Slack from The Prince's Foundation for Children & The Arts, both for the help they have given me in making this book happen, and for all of the fantastic work they do to introduce classical music to new listeners.

Index of Composers

About the Author

Darren Henley began reading the news at his local radio station, Invicta FM in Kent, when he was sixteen years old. Three years later, in 1992, he started working at Classic FM, the world's biggest classical music radio station, as a newsreader. His jobs there since then have included Managing Editor, Station Manager and Managing Director. Over the years, his radio programmes have won all sorts of awards, including one from the United Nations. He has written eighteen books about music and musicians, including a series of five *Classic FM Friendly Guides*, published by Hodder Education. He is also the Chairman of the Music Manifesto Partnership and Advocacy Group. The Music Manifesto campaigns to provide more opportunities for young people to live musical lives. Find out more at www.musicmanifesto.co.uk

The Prince's Foundation for
Children & the Arts

The Prince's Foundation for Children &
the Arts is an educational charity that helps
children experience the arts in a high
quality and sustained way. We provide
access for young people who would
otherwise grow up having had no, or very
limited, opportunity to engage with the
arts.

By buying this book you are helping to
fund our MusicQuest project. MusicQuest
takes classical musicians into schools and
theatres. Each year MusicQuest – with
funding from Classic FM Music Makers
and instruments and practical support
provided by Yamaha – introduces around
5,000 young people between the ages of 7
and 11 to the wonders of classical
orchestral music.

Classical music is surrounded with such
mystique that it can be hard to find out
what you enjoy . . . and what you don't.
You have to fight through the obscure
jargon and the lists of composers,
conductors, soloists, orchestras.

All of this can start to interfere with your quest to find and enjoy what, at the end of the day, is simply great music. We hope that MusicQuest will leave children involved with a life-long love of classical music, and perhaps encourage them to take up an instrument themselves.

With funding raised by Classic FM's charity, Classic FM MusicMakers, and instruments and practical support provided by Yamaha, MusicQuest is making a huge difference. Thank you for helping us to make MusicQuest possible by buying this book.